HAVE YOU SEEN MY DADDY?

HAVE YOU SEEN MY DADDY?

By Pastor John R. Peyton

My great-grandfather was a slave from Gambia, West Africa. He was purchased by a bridge at Fort Monroe in Hampton, Virginia. The five brothers were named Peyton, and one was John Peyton.

XULON PRESS

Xulon Press
2301 Lucien Way #415
Maitland, FL 32751
407.339.4217
www.xulonpress.com

Paperback ISBN-13: 978-1-6322-1086-9
Hard Cover ISBN-13: 978-1-6322-1087-6
Ebook ISBN-13: 978-1-6322-1088-3

My wife and I were at a fifth-grade parent-teacher meeting of our oldest daughter. As we walked around the classroom, looking at the projects and items the students had made, something grabbed my attention out of the corner of my eye. On one of the classroom bulletin boards, there were a number of things drawn and written by these young children. There was one poem that gripped my heart and has never left my mind and, most of all, my spirit ever since.

To the undiscerning eye, it would seem to be a simple three-stanza poem written by a fifth-grader. A simple poem handwritten by the hand of a child:

Daddy, Daddy, don't go away, would you, could you, please, please stay?
Daddy, Daddy, don't go away. I'll take your car keys to make you stay.
Daddy, Daddy, don't go away, would you, could you, please, please stay?

To the discerning eye, it was so much more than just a poem. It was the heartfelt cry of a child asking the question, which is the title of this book. This book may seem, to some, to be fragmented pieces of a man's life who is grateful, and is now able to answer the question: **HAVE YOU SEEN MY DADDY?** Come journey with me as I share how my earthly father wasn't in my daily life adventures, but my heavenly daddy was watching over me.

Daddy, Daddy, don't go away, would you,
could you, please, please stay

Daddy, Daddy, don't go away.

I'll take your car keys to make you stay

Daddy, Daddy, don't go away,

would you, could you, please, p'
stay.

OUR ART CORNER

Mrs. Jones
Rm. 9

DADDY, DADDY, DON'T GO AWAY, WOULD YOU,
COULD YOU, PLEASE, PLEASE STAY
DADDY, DADDY, DO GO AWAY.
I'LL TAKE YOUR CAR KEYS TO MAKE YOU STAY
DADDY, DADDY, DON'T GO AWAY.
WOULD YOU, COULD YOU, PLEASE, PLEASE STAY

This book is dedicated to my wife, Marie,
who stepped out in faith with me on a journey
and our three daughters (Wanda, Lorraine, Jessica),
and all the grandchildren, great-grandchildren,
staff, RCC, and friends.

Thanks to my proofreaders:
Mrs. Diane Lee and Dr. Carol Powell

TABLE OF CONTENTS

Chapter One

IN THE BEGINNING

My name is John Roger Peyton and I was born in 1946 to John Thomas and Elise Peyton. I was raised on Bethel Avenue (off Rip Rap Road) in Hampton, Virginia, in a home that had a coal/wood-burning stove in the dining room and a flat cook stove, which used coal and wood in the kitchen. We would cut wood for the stoves and go to the railroad track, which was about a half mile from my home, and get the coal that fell off the trains that passed daily through my neighborhood. I can remember collecting armloads of the coal and bringing it home in my little red wagon, so it could be used to warm our house and cook our meals. I was blessed to grow up with an older brother, two older sisters, and one younger brother. My mother also raised foster children. There was one boy that came to our house, and a year later my sister Doris and her family returned from overseas in the military and saw one of the foster children and confirmed to my mother's he was her own grandson by my oldest brother Albert. Another young boy came to spend the night and stayed with us until he was an adult.

My neighborhood was predominantly black Americans, and we were happy among ourselves. We owned our own stores, taxicab companies, restaurants, hotels, banks, dry cleaners, our own business college, etc. There was an appreciation for the Jewish people who didn't live in our neighborhood, but allowed black families to have credit at their stores and treated us with respect. One Jewish widow, Mrs. Roundtree had me cutting her yard, cleaning her flower beds, and washing her windows. Mrs. Roundtree was part-owner of the family furniture store. One day, her maid, Mrs. Bryant, was off duty and Mrs. Roundtree called me into the house and asked me to distribute her food. She left on her kitchen countertop a delicious-looking steak for Misty, the white poodle of the house, and a bologna sandwich for the yard caretaker, me. When she turned the corner, Misty got the bologna sandwich and I ate the steak. Poor Misty!

My father, John Thomas Peyton, was a boiler mechanic at Fort Monroe Army Base. He would turn into a monster on paydays and come home to physically and verbally assault my mother. We would try to help her, but he would threaten us with his gun. We would all have to run to my Aunt Maria's house to avoid the bullets that whizzed by our heads until he sobered up. When drunk my father would grab his guitar and sing a song, "The Eagle (money) Flies On Friday, Saturday I Go out to Play." Another of his favorite songs he sang was, "I Got A Woman (girlfriend) Way Over Town, and She's Good To Me." During the week, however, he would be a gentle giant, nice and kind.

I hated paydays. My father was weakened by alcohol, and when drunk, he would insult the family and spend the weekends with other women, coming home broke on Monday.

When I was about twelve, I enjoyed selling magazines (Jet, Ebony, Tan, Afro American, etc.), cleaning homes, and taking rags and metals to the junkyard. I would give my money to my mother to help pay the bills, and she would sometimes take me to the store to buy me a shiny new suit so I could be dressed nicely while in church on Sunday. I still like shiny suits. In our all black community, we would work together, share with our neighbors, and help each other through the wickedness and hardships that were put upon our community. I didn't realize it was purposeful, but it was the cards that life had dealt us.

I can remember cleaning the windows of rich people, especially the mayor of our town. His children would follow me throughout the house, because I would be singing and be very happy. These rich children were missing something because they seemed unhappy and unappreciative of all they had.

Known for my whistling and singing, people would come over to where I was working, listen, and give me money for making their day. At one point, I cleaned all the business store windows in my town. I was trusted into people's homes and businesses to clean them. I can remember looking back at my hard work to make sure when my mother came to inspect, with her freshly starched white gloves on, I could proudly say I did the job. I remember sneaking over to Mrs. Roundtree's house to throw some dirt on the big living room windows, just so I would get a call to come and wash them. She wanted them clean for her bridge club on Wednesdays. Some would say that was the beginning of my entrepreneurship.

Chapter Two

MY INTRODUCTION TO A WHITE JESUS, WHITE SANTA CLAUS, AND THE CHURCH

O ne of my fondest memories of my mother was hearing her singing hymns and gospel songs unto the Lord and hearing her playing the piano in the living room. Even when hanging clothes on the line, she would be rejoicing unto the Lord. I didn't realize then that my mother was worshipping and singing through her pain. I had a strong tenor voice, so I would sing along with her.

As a family, except for our father, we would regular attend Sunday school and church. If I played sick, I was given a tonic called castor oil, which was the worst taste one could ever encounter! I knew we would get it if we tried to get out of going to church.

I couldn't understand the church game. All the pictures in our King James Bible showed bible characters as being white. The picture of the Last Supper showed Jesus and His disciples and everyone was white. Nobody in my neighborhood was white, so I didn't understand this whitewashed Jesus. I also couldn't understand, when watching Superman, why there were no black people in Metropolis, even though it was fictional.

One Sunday morning, my best friend Victor and I slipped out of our church and went to the white church, which was fifty-eight steps from our church on North King Street in Hampton, Virginia. When we got to the front door of the church, we were told that n****rs weren't allowed. I can remember standing outside on the steps of that church, thinking to myself, what kind of heavenly streets were church people going to be walking on, when they can't walk together on earthly streets?

I came to the conclusion that Jesus was white, Santa Claus was white, and all the people in the King James Bible were white. That made me feel left out. That jolly white Santa Claus (at Leggett's Department Store) with the white beard never gave me the toys that I sat on his lap and asked for, so I figured that the white Jesus was a liar also. No white man was coming down our chimney Christmas, because we didn't have a fireplace, but there would be a red-hot stove was waiting for him. I saw so much hypocrisy in the church growing up that my experiences shaped my negative thinking at a young age about the church and Christianity.

One example of church hypocrisy that I observed in my youth was that women were not allowed to stand on the stage in the church behind the pulpit. Those who had been out drinking and partying all Saturday night at the clubs would be up there, in robes, singing in the choir. The active, homosexual choir leader, adulteress and fornicators were allowed to direct the choir. It all seemed like a joke to me.

I was fifteen when leaders of the church adult choir came and asked my mother if I could sing with them. We walked past my church every day on our way to high school, which was three miles away. When I went to the first rehearsal, I was told by an adult choir member that I had to go through an initiation to become a part of the choir.

After rehearsal, they took my best friend Victor and me to one of the adults' houses and we were given liquor to drink. We were told by these adults' playing cards that we had to play a game to get accepted into the choir. We had to take off all our clothes, go into a dark room, and what happened next was my introduction to having sex with older women. This turned on a sexual addiction within me that I was able to overcome as an adult with Christ in my life. I never thought I could tell my mother what happened, because I figured she wouldn't believe me. In those days, adults were always right, even though some were bald-faced liars. These people were "going to hell though the church." I just thought Christianity was a joke and the choir members didn't fear God. There was adultery everywhere in the church; one example of this was when I went downstairs at church to the bathroom, while the pastor was preaching, and saw two women fighting about messing with another's husband. I just didn't know what to think! We would go on church trips and some adults would have brown bags with whiskey bottles, which they would drink before we sang. Meanwhile, my mother and my god-mother were honest believers, trying to serve the Lord.

Even in the midst of all of this, I was still fine-tuning my entrepreneur skills. I was selling magazines, while picking up iron, tin, and clothes to sell at the junkyard. I did this to buy my mother appliances that she needed. I would by-pass the pool hall and other gambling spots, and proudly take my money to the store to buy my mom a blender, floor buffer, vacuum cleaner, window air conditioner unit, clothes, and the latest gadgets. I am still a gadget man today.

I loved my mom very much and would watch her smile, sometimes with black eyes covered by sunglasses after a bad weekend with my father. Every morning, she directed traffic at the school and was the first female black safety guard. People were so touched by her morning smile, that our car would be full of gifts from the drivers, especially during Christmas time. I learned from my mom to smile even in the midst of heartache, turmoil, and devastating pain. I remember once when my father was living in Norfolk, Virginia for over a year because of a job transfer. Everything needed fell on my mother to provide for the family because of the absence of my father. Once we didn't have any food in the house. Mother set the table and we were sitting there, with no food. Mom prayed a powerful prayer! Soon there came a knock at our back door and Mrs. Elizabeth, our neighbor had a big bowl of spaghetti. She said the Lord told her to bring this to our house. My mother was a woman of faith and really trusted this man Jesus! I saw many miracles like this in my mother's life.

I can remember in the first grade making my teacher, Mrs. Margaret Phillips, very upset and nervous. She asked my mother to set me up for a beating. I remember my mother saying (on Saturday morning) she wanted to play cowboy with me, which we played all the time, so like always I would let her tie me up to the tree and I would always get loosed. I let her tie me up to a tree. This one time I noticed she went around the tree with the rope quite a few extra times. Next thing I know, Mrs. Phillips drove up and gave me a beating while tied to the tree in my yard. My reputation for talking too much preceded me. As a matter of fact, one fifth-grade teacher refused to let me be promoted to her class. She had taught my daddy and swore she would never teach another person named John Peyton.

My mother was hired as the first black school police guard when I was in elementary (Union Elementary) and was transferred to my middle school (Y. H. Thomas) and my high school (George P. Phenix). She was placed at the schools to help shape up my behavior.

When it came to schoolwork, I didn't make good grades. The only time I did was if the teacher said I needed an "A" to pass the class. I would study and get an "A" every time, because a "D" was passing during my school years. Unless I got an "A" on my final exam, the teacher said I wouldn't pass the class. That would kick me into gear. Challenge on!!! Challenge accomplished!!!

Chapter Three

WHO I REALLY AM

I am a charismatic personality with a burst of energy; I genuinely love people. Even as a child, I would get creative ideas and take over the leadership of whatever was happening. I have to laugh now at myself, as I remember staring up in the air around the flag pole in the morning while students gathered and before you knew it, everyone was staring up with me, asking what I was looking at. I once took a coat hanger and shaped it to look like I had an invisible animal with me and everyone was interested in my invisible dog. They were following me around; everyone except the principal, Mr. Hill. He did not find the humor in it at all and gave me some days home to spend with my invisible dog.

You would think being suspended from school would have taught me to temper my mischievousness, but it didn't. I got into more trouble during a two-day suspension by riding around the school grounds on my grandfather's donkey. Of course, I made sure I was riding right in the view of everyone so everyone was out of their seats at the windows watching me. My reward was another beating with switches (branches tied together) and having my mouth washed out with a wash rag and Ivory soap, which was normal punishment for me. I hate Ivory soap to this day. When caught by adults using profanity, Mother would hear about it and wait until I was asleep with my mouth open. I was awakened, gasping for breath with the rag swirling around inside my mouth and my mother declaring, "I bet you won't cuss anymore."

For the record, I didn't set my seventh grade class files on fire, but I was the first suspect because I had been caught in the past, in the back of the class, sneaking and smoking cigarettes. Fortunately, it was proven this time that I was at home. My father was drunk when he came to my middle school to beat me in front of the class, for getting caught smoking after they repaired the classroom. He had about fifteen switches platted up and was determined to publicly beat me.

My favorite teacher, Mrs. McDonald, begged my father not to do it and he was dismissed from the grounds. I thought I had weathered that storm, but when I arrived home and I didn't see his truck, I went into the house and immediately received the beaten of a lifetime.

In my spare time, I did like to throw rocks at abandoned autos and vacant homes in the city. Throwing rocks was a release and fun. I remember my neighbor Lewis Johnson calling me "Black!!" (bad word during my days). I threw a rock at him, and that rock slowly left my hand and gracefully sailed a few yards from me toward Lewis. I had a smile on my lips, as I knew it was going to land right at Lewis's big head. Lewis then did the unthinkable. You got it...Lewis ducked. My smile disappeared. That rock went right into what was just behind him, his mother's Volkswagen, and, more precisely, his mother's front-glass window. Boy, did I get a beating and I had to pay my father back for having the window fixed.

When growing up, I was tall and skinny for my age. I was able to unscrew the bulbs on people's porches and I got great humor out of seeing people attempting to turn on their porchlights at dusk, only to find they had been unscrewed. I love people too much to hurt them physically and verbally. I would do little mischievous things instead, but because those in the neighborhood knew I really did love them and wouldn't hurt them, and they loved me. They would simply give my mother a phone call and tell her, "Elsie, that little rascal of yours has done it again!"

It was during ninth grade when I met my childhood sweetheart, Marie Addie Dennis. She and her family moved into our community and was one street from us on Parkside Avenue. Her parents were hard workers. Her father worked for a white owned dry cleaning business during the day and was a bartender during the night until around midnight. Her mother ran the family owned dry cleaner. Both worked long hours. The street they lived on was paved, while my street still was a dirt road. Their bathroom had a toilet in the house, while ours was an outhouse in the backyard. She was a beautiful, smart seventh-grader when we met, while I was what they called "a hoodlum." We met each other playing football in her yard and fell in love as teens.

Marie had the ability to keep me calm and convinced me not to be over the top, doing crazy things when I became angry. It was the same thing my mom could do. Marie and I were with each other almost every day, as I helped her deliver the dry-cleaned clothes for her mother and she would watch me wash windows. When we would get into trouble, our parents restricted us from calling each other on the home phone. Instead, we would have conversations on walkie talkies that I brought and we would talk through the night.

When it was time to graduate from high school in 1964, everyone in the family was nervous because I was behind in all my classes, except choir because I loved to sing. The only way I could graduate was to get all A's on my final exams. Challenge on!! So, I accepted the challenge to get "A's" on all my final exams in order to pass and graduate. Challenge won!!!

Even though my name was on the list to graduate, the principal, Mr. Stevenson, found out that we had set up a dance club under the auditorium's stage, which was supposed to be used for storage for the football equipment only. Well, we had turned it into a little spot for dancing and where students would hang out when skipping class. Although Mr. Stevenson wanted to use this opportunity to nail me, no teacher wanted to have me in his/her class for another year. So, I was socially promoted. Social promotion is the practice of promoting a student to the next grade after the current school year, regardless if he/she learned the necessary material or not. That was me.

John And Marie's High School Prom

Chapter Four

GOING INTO THE MILITARY...HOW THE MILITARY SAVED MY LIFE

After graduation, my mother gave me two options – go into the military or go to college. There was no sitting at home. I decided to go to a local business college; the Peninsula Business College, attended mainly by girls. This school was not recognized as an accredited college. I got into classes that taught administrative skills and ended up in a typing class. We had typing races on a Royal typewriter. Challenge on!!! I ended up typing up to 125 wpm. Challenge won!!!

I was just having a fun time when Mom called me at my Marie's house and told me she had a special letter for me. I ran home, all excited to see this letter for me. As I opened it, the first words I read were, "Greetings, you have been drafted into the United States Armed Forces."

I was devastated. I screamed out that I didn't want to be in the white man's army. "Momma, they are going to send me to Vietnam and get me killed!" My mother looked at me and said, "John Roger, I will be praying for you." I've always believed, to this day, that Mother turned my name into the government, because our uncle, Gibbs Carter, was a career soldier and she thought it would be best for me to go into the military. She told me that if I would volunteer to go in for an extra year, I surely wouldn't go to Vietnam. Unfortunately, Mother didn't know the system, but she did know God.

It was 1965 and I remember having a heavy heart, and a bit of anger, while sadly getting on the bus to go to Fort Jackson in Columbia, South Carolina. I arrived with a few clothes, personal items, and a small New Testament Bible given to me by my mother. I had no idea what was going to happen. I was standing with other recruits, in the dark, smoking a cigarette. Suddenly, Sergeant Mongo, our drill sergeant, came and acted so nice to us. He introduced himself and told us to follow him. We went into this building and he told us to raise our hands to be sworn into the United States Army. We all raised our hands, and as soon as we said the words of commitment, this man with the kind words started screaming at us and made us go back outside in the dark and pick up all the cigarette butts we had been smoking outside. This big, black, 6'4" tall man then proceeded screaming at us, "For the next eight weeks, I am going to be your parents, your momma, your daddy, and your sweet-hearts!!" A new adventure began.

We were marched to the barbershop. When I stepped in, one of the barbers asked me how I would like my big afro trimmed. After giving him some delicate directions of just take a little off the top, the next thing I knew he took off all the hair in the middle of my head and proceeded all around my head. I was bald in a matter of minutes, and then Sergeant Mongo shaved the sixteen hairs off my face.

That crazy sergeant marched and ran us everywhere, and sometimes he was riding in his jeep as we ran behind him. He caught me talking in the chow line, so I had to stand outside the chow line and holler, "I love to talk"; and about an hour later, I had to holler, "I talk too much." It was crazy! A few days later, I caught a white boy peeping while I showered, and I was about to beat him to the ground. He told me he was told I had a tail like a monkey. After having all my fellow black comrades come in the shower to prove we weren't monkeys with tails, he just cried and said his parent taught him that.

Eight weeks later, I graduated basic training with my chest poked out, and with senses of accomplishment and pride. God knows all of us were different men than those high school boys who had arrived two months earlier. I didn't realize it at the time, but Sergeant Mongo was preparing me for one of the greatest fights of my life.

It was in basic training that I learned how to use a weapon and how to survive, in addition to the survival skills I learned growing up in our neighborhood.

After graduation, I was sent to administrative school and shipped out to Fort Lee in Petersburg, Virginia. I thought, at this point, I had surely dodged the bullet called Vietnam.

One Friday night at Fort Lee in Petersburg, Virginia, I was leaning out of my barrack's window and a fellow soldier who was buffing the floor ran across my heel. He severed my Achilles tendon and blood was everywhere, as I went berserk. I had big plans for the weekend of going to Hampton to see my girlfriend Marie, but I had to have surgery instead. They told me I wouldn't be walking for a long time. I would place myself at the bottom of my bed and most of the night, I would be trying to get my foot strong again by pushing it against the bed post. Before I knew it, I could walk strongly again. I didn't want it known about my miraculous recovery, so I would walk around on crutches during the day and be dancing in the barracks at night. One night, my commanding officer caught me dancing and I was given orders to go to the Panama Canal, Fort Amador, where I was assigned to be a clerk, because I could type very fast. I was eventually moved up to Quarry Heights, where the top commanders were.

During my time in Panama, I met some Black Panther brothers who felt like I did about the white man, but to a greater level. They also believed in the ideology of the Black Panther Party. We needed to know the strategy of top military whites, so I was learning from what I typed, the very mind of the white man's army, in preparation for the black people's "revolution."

It was the white man's insecurity that caused him to learn to advance through the black people's knowledge. As soon as the white man gets your knowledge, he would steal it, destroy you, and take credit for all your brilliancy. I have always believed that the greatest ideal of the white man was the ownership of the patent office. Many people have had their inventions stolen. I have since learned from my own research this belief I have always believed to be true. Shontavia Johnson, who is a lawyer and professor of Intellectual Property Law at Drake University, wrote a powerful piece on how historically African American slaves being denied (or having outright stolen), patents for their inventions. Johnson writes, "One group of prolific innovators, however, has been largely ignored by history: black inventors born or forced into American slavery. Though U.S. patent law was created with color-blind language to foster innovation, the patent system consistently excluded these inventors from recognition." She goes to explain that the patent system, which officially started in 1787, was not accessible or open to African Americans born into slavery as they weren't considered citizens.

Oh, how I hated white men and would verbally describe them in such a way that other black men wanted to destroy them. I was soon a lieutenant in the Black Panther ideology.

Being the only black in my office, I was watching the games people played to get rank, by running around sexually with other people. There was this one sergeant that didn't just go to church but brought the church to work with him. We would all give him hell and the dirty work. Many others in the office went to church, but I guess after the benediction, they put Jesus on the shelf, like those in the church where I grew up. Sergeant Lloyd Sheets just kept being a convicting light unto my soul, while I was plotting on how to kill white people. I just couldn't think that way about Sgt. Lloyd Sheets. He reminded me of my righteous mother, and his kindness was surely getting on my nerves with his Jesus talk and sharing his wife's banana cake with me. I was telling my brothers in the Black Panther Party how his kindness was getting on my last nerve.

"Your life might be the only Bible some people will ever read!" (Quote from William J. Toms, farmer and Methodist leader, Blisland, Cornwall England.)

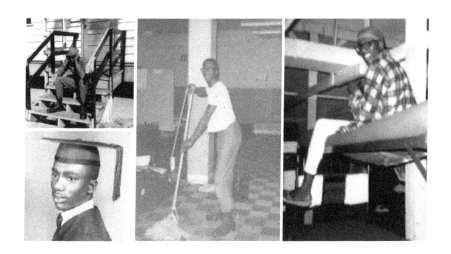

Chapter Five

GETTING BORN AGAIN...WE DIDN'T JUST CATCH A FISH! WE CAUGHT A WHALE!!!

I t was 1966 when Sergeant Sheets asked me, during lunch, if I would attend his church off base on Friday night. I told him that blacks and whites don't go into the same church building; he told me that they did at his church in Paraiso which was downtown in the Canal Zone. I said, "Man, I never saw it in my hometown of Hampton, Virginia, growing up."

So, I decided I just wanted to see it for myself. I told him I would stay about thirty minutes, then head out and go to the Rancho night-club, hoping this favor would get him out of my life. I didn't know he and others had been praying for my soul.

I told him I didn't want to be seen with him, so we agreed to meet when the sun went down. I would crawl into the back seat of his car, lay down on the floor, ride to the church, and get back to base in a cab. He swore he wouldn't tell anyone. I was looking forward to getting this over and getting back to doing my stirring messages against the white man at our Black Panther headquarters we had off base. Whites had to die during our "revolution."

We got to the church and for the first time, I saw blacks, Panamanians, and white Americans in the same building in Paraiso. Paraiso is a town in the Republic of Panama, located just north of the Panama Canal. As we entered the church, I sat in the back, waiting for my chance to make a break for the door. They were singing songs with such joy (Power in the Blood) and tears were coming down their faces. I was hoping to get out the door, but Pastor Millard Cowdell got up and said, **"Somebody is going to hell."** I decided to listen just a few more minutes because I told my mother that most of the people in our church were going to hell with me. I stayed and heard the whole sermon and before I knew it, he was asking for those who needed prayer to come to the front. I knew I needed prayer and found myself coming up to the front of the church.

Next thing I knew, I was fighting my flesh over my hate for whites, the nightclub where I loved to go to dance and drink, the pint of Jim Beam in my pocket, and the women I was on my way to party with. I was a lover of cussing and being nasty to white people. I was in the fight of my life on my knees at that church altar. I could hear people praying and Pastor Cowdell saying, "Touch him Lord, touch him!" I remember hands pressing down on my head and all I could think, as I wrestled in my spirit, was that they were messing up my afro. Next thing I knew, a fellow army soldier, Tom Netherton, future singer on *The Lawrence Welk Show,* and I were praying to receive Christ into our hearts. The Holy Ghost came upon us, and we were crying and speaking in new tongues. I was so changed in my heart and flesh that I put on the pulpit my pack of Pall Mall cigarettes, pint of Jim Beam, a marijuana joint, switch blade pocket knife, my Black Panther arm bands, and my filthy way of communicating, as the joy of the Lord came into my heart, soul, and mind. As I laid all of those items on the altar of that small church in Panama, I remember hearing Pastor Cowdell shout out, "We didn't catch a fish; we just caught a whale!!!" I had never been happier in my life. The Holy Ghost is real when you repent and invite Jesus into your heart. You can't be pure in the head....you must be pure in the heart.

When you really get saved (don't knock it until you try it), you're in no hurry to leave the fire you discover in the fellowship. I just had to go and tell my comrades, who were waiting for me to come speak my nasty points of view and ideology against the white man, about the change that had happened inside of me. When I arrived, I signaled for everyone to be quiet. Everyone settled down, ready to hear my rhetoric, but instead I began to share, as tears came down my face, how I had just invited Jesus Christ into my life, and that I loved everybody and wanted to tell everybody about Jesus Christ, the Savior. I left our party's headquarters without a knife being put into my back and returned back to my barrack to live my life for Christ.

This new life was difficult, for I was laughed and mocked at when I would kneel by my bed and pray at night. I would hear snickering and called names that I would have stabbed a person for, but my life was so changed by the Lord that I went to every Bible study the church had and I was not cussing anymore. I noticed when the light went off in the barracks, I could hear other men getting out of their beds praying before sleeping. Many later went to church with me, including a comrade who tried to put a knife in my back the night I left the room after sharing with my comrades my commitment to Christ. He said there was a wall around me, protecting me. Real Christian fellowship is contagious, to where you just can't wait to come together with fellow believers.

After just receiving Christ into my life, I received news that my father had shot my older brother in the back and they weren't sure he was going to live. The devil spoke and told me I needed to go home and kill him. The devil reminded me of all the beatings my mother had taken, all the abuse we had suffered at his hand, and now he had shot my brother. However, the Holy Ghost told me to go to the church and get with Pastor Cowdell to pray. I left Quarry Heights with permission and went to the church instead of trying to get the Red Cross to send me home. When I gave it to Jesus, my burden was released. My brother survived the shooting and after getting better, he left home and we nor his wife and children have never been in contact with him again.

Months later, with no animosity, I went back to my hometown to see my family and girlfriend, Marie. My parents didn't know I was coming home and when I jumped over the home fence with my duffle bag, my father, who was working in the yard, spotted me, and looked terrified. I dropped my duffle bag, bent over to my father, and just hugged him. I started telling everyone about the change in my life. I also decided that I wanted to marry Marie and return back with her to Panama.

I proposed to Marie in Williamsburg, Virginia, as we sat on a dock fishing. I remember that day like yesterday, as my childhood friend and sweetheart jumped up, throwing the fishing pole into the water, and said, "Yes." I was a happy, young man. Sgt. Sheets helped me with the military papers, after asking Marie's parents to marry her and getting permission. Marie and I had our simple wedding on the front steps of her grandfather's house. We then went to a hotel and watched the Pink Panther movie, and just couldn't believe we were now married and didn't have to answer to anybody. I now had another responsibility.

For our honeymoon, my new wife's father, Mr. Dennis, wanted to pay for our week at the hotel. I told him he could pay up until Thursday and I would take care from there, because I was a man. Well, on Friday morning, my wife and I woke up and she wanted breakfast. We had been feasting on lobster tails, steak, and baked potatoes all week long, but today was Friday, my time to take over. I said to my new bride, "Girl, I got you covered." I got up, dressed, and went to McDonald's and that is how we started our marriage.

God provided for us to get Marie's passport and all the shots she needed to return with me to Panama to start our lives as husband and wife. We were given housing on Quarry Heights, where low-rank enlisted men, like me, weren't allowed to have housing. We were given the grace of God, and it was a miraculous beginning.

We had so much fun going to church during the week and having miraculous Sunday services. Three months into our marriage, Marie had a miscarriage that was painful and then someone broke into our apartment while at church. We searched to see what was missing, but the only thing taken was my favorite box of ginger snaps.

John And Marie: Our Wedding Day

Chapter Six

VIETNAM AND BACK TO
MY HOMETOWN

I t was found out who and what I was about in the army after my conversion, and a special order from the Pentagon came for me to go to
Vietnam. That was 1967 and we tried everything to get it reversed. Now
I had to take Marie back to her parents' house in Virginia. As I was on
my way to be shipped out of the country, I stopped in Seattle to visit my
best friend, Victor, in the military. He shared with me about his latest
pleasure, shooting heroin into his arms. I shared my newfound faith
and told him I was determined to serve the Lord. I kept telling him
and another soldier that Jesus was the answer. His buddy was trying
to jump from the twelfth floor balcony because the heroin was telling
him he could fly. I was up all night ministering the Word of God to
both of them.

The next day, I left Seattle and many hours later, I found myself
landing in Saigon, Vietnam during the 1967 December Tet Offensive.
We were being fired upon as our C-130 plane, landed in Saigon and my
life was entirely in the hands of God. I saw death all around me and one
night, I missed a certain death. An old Vietnamese woman told me to
get in the bunker before 8pm because many bombs would be coming
onto our base. She liked my disposition and I always treated her with

25

respect. I was in the bunker at 6pm and, sure enough, we were hit and many died.

I had many near-death experiences. I thank God for keeping me. I didn't have to drink, smoke drugs, or have sex with young women to find relief. My relief came in having a relationship with Jesus Christ.

I couldn't believe how our Christian nation treated other human beings that were trapped in a winless war. I remember one day, while on patrol in Nha Tran, we ran across a mother and daughter bent over in the rice paddy. Some of the men decided to snatch and rape them. I refused to participate in such sickness. I was asked to sit on the hill and be the watch-out person, in case some Viet Cong should come along. I just began to pray that the two women would lift up their heads and see them sneaking up on them. All of a sudden, God touched the mother, and she spotted them and the two took off running. I prayed that God would give them swiftness, and they escaped and outran the soldiers. God heard my prayer and I was rejoicing in my heart. If you wonder why I didn't object, I wouldn't be typing this book. I think rape is a great violation upon a woman. Some of my friends were attempting to rape a girl during a church service and I helped her escape unharmed. I met her many years later, and she recognized me and again thanked me in the presence of her husband and children. **"People may forget what you said or what you did, but not how you made them feel."**

After six months of stress in Vietnam, we were sent to Bangkok for one week of rest and relaxation. It was good to be off the battlefield. Many of my comrades were paying women to be with them while there. I just sat in my hotel room, praying, and the Lord led me to a store, where I found out the owner and his whole family were believers in Jesus Christ. I was in their house church every day and learned that God has His people everywhere. I returned back to Vietnam with a strong faith and determination to get back home and serve the Lord all the days of my life.

Soldiers were again allowed a weekend off of the battlefield, and a few of us believers found in Saigon a missionary couple, Mom and Pop Kincaid, who fixed us a great meal and prayed over us. There was fighting in the streets around the house, but they weren't harmed while in Vietnam.

I returned home in 1968 and landed in California first before flying to Virginia. I was shocked at how women had their dresses high above their knees. I was so glad to see my wife and mother, and tell my family about the goodness of the Lord. It took me a few days to relax and gather my mind and heart, knowing that I was safe again. I had to spend a few days not being close to my wife, because my reflex was to shove the nose bone up her face when she went to hug me as a surprise. We lived on the edge for a little time. Going to war is not easy on any soldier, no matter what position he/she plays on the team. My peace of mind comes from trusting Jesus as my Lord.

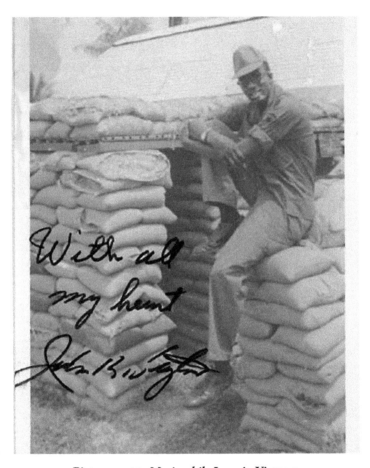

Picture sent to Marie while I was in Vietnam

Chapter Seven

I AM BROKE?

After spending a week with my in-laws, I kept asking Marie how much money we saved by me sending home all my paychecks, except $50.00 a month in Vietnam. My father-in-law sat me down and informed me that my wife didn't save any of the money I was sending home, and he offered me a large check to get us started because he never taught her to be financially responsible. My pride wouldn't let me take it, so with my new wife, we moved into a low-income neighborhood and I was working any job I could to take care of my family. I worked construction, cleaned offices, washed windows, cut grass, cleaned homes and schools, or whatever I could find that was honest work. When you are used to being responsible, it's easy to go and make honest money.

I sold vacuum cleaners and finally landed a job selling Metropolitan Life Insurance. I never realized how hard it was to convince a family that they needed life insurance, in case of the early death of one of the spouses, and how the company could guarantee money for burial, children's college, and continual income for the home. I had to go and collect the premiums from people so they wouldn't be late on their payments, and in some cases, visit people at their jobs when they got paid. I found myself knocking on doors, canvassing during the day, and selling policies at night when both husband and wife were home. As I was trying to be one of the best, another salesman, George Provost, convinced me to go to Norfolk State College and take the entrance exam, using my

GI Bill money for college. At twenty-two years of age, I thought I was too old and not smart enough to get a BS degree, but he talked me into it. I took the entrance exam, only to find I wasn't up to the educational criteria to get into the college. I would have to take eighteen non-credit courses before I could get started on my first year of college.

God again showed up, because a retired, white schoolteacher stopped by the historical black college and told the president that she was willing to help anyone with reading and comprehension problems. He told me about the lady and I immediately got in touch with her. She agreed to help me to read fast with comprehension. To this day, I am a still a speed reader. She helped many students to get on the road of graduating from the college.

I went to college during the day and found a night job at Newport News Shipyard as a steel stamper. God knows it wasn't an easy job, because when the steel was cut, and still hot, I had to get on my knees and put the information about where the steel pieces fit on the ship with alphabetical steel stencils while the material was red hot. There was no time for a mistake or I would end up with third-degree burns. I was averaging around four hours of sleep daily. My college counselor said it would take me six years to finish my degree in business management. Would you believe that God blessed me to graduate from Norfolk State University in four years? My school counselor was amazed to see my name to graduate so early. I went to college classes during the whole year and many days, I don't remember some days driving through the Norfolk, Virginia tunnel, but surely the Lord had His hand upon my life and determination. My shipyard co-workers were so proud about what I was trying to do that they would help me to find time to study, hiding me behind boxes so I could study during our one-hour lunch. They always encouraged me to finish college, because it was something they didn't get the chance to do.

I started a Bible study during lunch break in the shipyard and ended up with at least sixty people in attendance. Many became ministers, deacons, and pastors. God is so good! Others started leading the Bible study and they all pledged to come to my college graduation.

As time rolled on, along with the shipyard work and college, I found myself having a weekend job as a security guard for NASA at Langley Air Force Base, teaching a young adult Sunday school class, and being the leader of a gospel group. We would sing at the homes of people who were sick or shut-in, nursing homes and at the VA hospital for veterans.

Chapter Eight

BUYING OUR FIRST HOME

M arie and I also applied for Section 8 housing using my GI ben-efits. We ended up in a brand-new neighborhood with twenty homes in Phoebus, Virginia, where most of the homes were being occu-pied by people who had come from city projects. To keep up the value of our homes, we had the children and parents in the neighborhood sitting in front of our house on Friday nights, singing unto the Lord and watching Christian movies (*Thief in the Night*, etc....). I remember one Friday night, while we were watching a movie, two single-parent mothers got into a fight in the middle of the street near where we were showing the movie. I stood up and asked all the kids, including those whose parents were fighting, to come where I was standing. We joined hands and, on our knees, we prayed even as the fight was going on.

The mothers were so embarrassed and convicted they stopped fighting, apologized, hugged one another, and promised to never do that again. That was the beginning of our Neighborhood Community Action Committee. We were blessed to have neighborhood clean-up, lessons on how to wash windows, cut grass, and plant flowers and shrubs. We became a beautiful and peaceful neighborhood. Many youths from other neighborhoods came to our neighborhood to watch movies and be taught how to be kind to one another. We had no bullies in our community.

I challenged the mothers on welfare to come and ride in my van to the shipyard to get jobs. They did and eventually got off welfare. I had thirteen women going with me into the shipyard every day, and we had a clean, blessed neighborhood on Georgianna Court in Phoebus, Virginia. As we went to work every day, we would sing: "Long as I have shoes to put on my feet and food for my children to eat, everything is going to be alright, be alright, everything is going to be alright." We read Scripture while riding to and from work. Eventually, the ladies drove themselves to work and loved being off that addictive welfare system.

In 1974, after seven years of marriage, Marie gave her life to Christ, was filled with the Holy Ghost, and we were finally on the same page concerning Christ as Lord.

Our Early Years

Chapter Nine

MY PAST CATCHES UP AND MY FUTURE AWAITS ME

My father was an oil burner mechanic on Fort Monroe Army Base in Hampton, Virginia. One day, he was asked to go and fix the furnace of a woman that liked to talk about Jesus. Nobody wanted to go, but my father said he would, because his son was always talking about Jesus. After he fixed Sergeant and Mrs. Eckert's boiler, she started talking about Jesus, and they talked about being in the Panama Canal zone. My dad said, "My son was there, too!" As they were talking, they asked for my father's name, which is the same as mine. They shared how they knew a new convert in the Canal Zone that had the same name as his and was sent to Vietnam, and how the church in Panama was praying for his safety.

They showed a picture of me and my dad, told them that I was his son, and that I lived less than five miles from their Fort Monroe home. They called and I met them. We rejoiced in the Lord with all our might; they had been praying for me!!! I didn't know they had been praying. They were still praying for that "whale" they had caught the night I got saved.

We shared about how Tom Netherton and I got saved the same night. Ruth Eckert happened to be the one who set up the guests for Pat Robertson's *700 Club* at that time. Next thing I knew, I was on the TV with Pat Robertson, giving my testimony. Doors really started opening for me to come and give my testimony at churches of all denominations.

One day, I received a call to come to a Baptist church in Norfolk, Virginia to give my testimony. I told the pastor I was not a preacher, but he was convinced God's anointing was upon me, after seeing me on the *700 Club*. The pastor told me that the deacons won't let me in the pulpit, unless I have a reverend in my title. I didn't have reverend in my title: the only titles I had was that of a husband, a father, and a servant of God. The pastor said he was going to put it on the program as Rev. John Peyton, so the youth of his church could hear my testimony. I went with my wife and family and the neighborhood gospel-singing group, consisting of the youth in our neighborhood.

After the young people had sung, the Spirit of God came upon that Baptist church in a mighty way. The atmosphere was set. I got up and as I started sharing my conversion to Jesus Christ, the heat and power of His Holy Spirit came upon me and before I knew it, I was declaring the Word of God with power and might. That dignified Baptist church had an Acts 2 experience!

Twenty-seven people gave their lives to Christ, and the pastor was jumping up and down, praising the Lord. He looked at me and said, "Pray for the sick." I was obedient and called for the sick and afflicted. A man rolled his mother down the aisle who had suffered a stroke. When I reached out and touched her, she jumped up out of the wheelchair, dancing and running, and her crooked hands straightened out. That service lasted until three-thirty pm, which was amazing because most Baptists are out by twelve-thirty pm. Surely the Lord was upon us. People lined up and down the aisles to be prayed over.

I left the church in shock; I had no words. The fifteen teenagers in my youth group and my family were all quiet in the van. No one said it, but we were all thinking, about *what just happened?* We knew it was God and we were all quiet.

As we were travelling down the highway, the Lord spoke, in an audible voice to me, "Preach the Word of God." I stopped the van and asked Marie to drive us home. I was having a life-changing experience like Paul had on the Road to Damascus in Acts 9. We are all called to minister and share the Gospel, but this was a specific call to preach, which to me meant full time ministry for the Lord.

We all went to my house and I ran to my prayer room. The youth singing group, who were with me in the van, came into my living room to pray with my wife and a preacher friend. This preacher friend led my wife to Christ. They found me in my prayer room and asked what I was going to do with the call from God on my life.

My friend Sam reminded me how just three weeks earlier, the prophet who was preaching called us out at the revival meeting. We were sitting in the service, laughing at how he was calling people up to him and they were falling on the floor. I jokingly told my friend that he was using knockout smoke under his sleeves. We sat there snickering and joking.

As we sat there watching, he called out a woman, Mrs. Brasswell, who we knew had problems walking, because we brought her and had to lift her up in our van to get her there. My friend and I looked at each other like, "We got him now!!!" We know Mrs. Brasswell!!! She wasn't a plant. We sat up on the edge of our seats and watched intently, as the prophet called her forward and started praying over her. To our amazement, Mrs. Brasswell started to run around the room, praising God with all her might. We were terrified for laughing and thinking it was a trick.

The prophet then had my friend Sam and me to stand right in front of the seats we were sitting in. He rebuked us for doubting him and for doubting that the Spirit of the Lord was upon him. He went on to say we would be powerful men in the hands of the Lord. He then said he wasn't going to touch us.

The last thing I remember was that he simply blew wind out of his mouth in our direction. I believe the Lord said, Challenge on!!! Marie told us later that my friend and I took out two rows of chairs when we were knocked out in the Spirit for thirty minutes. Challenge won by the Lord!!! I will never play with truly anointed people again.

Things in the ministry that the Lord had for me really started moving forward after that. My friend Sam went on to preach his first sermon and was licensed to be a preacher in the Baptist denomination. I also told my pastor about my decision to go into ministry. In the presence of my wife, he said that I was too serious about Christ and that I was embarrassing him. He didn't like me being on the streets sharing the gospel with people. He wasn't happy about the fact that I would mingle with people of all denominations.

It took the deacons and trustees of our local church to literally threaten him before he agreed to license me as a minister of the gospel. He called and told me, at the last minute, that on Sunday evening, I would be licensed and would preach my trial sermon, a term used in the Baptist denomination. You have to see the irony in this being done on a Sunday evening, because our church had never had a Sunday evening service. He did this hoping that others wouldn't attend, but word got out and it looked like our whole town came out. The pulpit was filled with pastors. They all rejoiced over my calling, which many said they had seen it in me for a long time.

My first sermon was, *"Jesus the Trash Collector"* (Isa. 64:6), because I had discovered that all our righteousness was filthy rags to Jesus. The church was packed. When people started verbally praising the Lord, the pastor got up and stopped me. In the middle of the sermon, he said if there were any more emotional outbursts, he would stop my preaching again. Everyone sat down after this and I was licensed . . . but the call upon my life had already been sealed by God.

I continued to do shows for Pat Robertson. Was in the room when we prayed over the mail that would make *the 700 Club* be launched into the stations, as you see it today. I was also with the young Jim and Tammy Faye Bakker before they went onto the national scene, and other beautiful people Sister Ruth Eckert introduced me to.

I just wanted to be one of Jesus's disciples, but the organized church was trying to hold me back. I discovered early that I can sell Jesus, but it's hard to sell people into His Church!

My family . . . has been with me every step of the way.

OUR GIRLS

Our Daughters

Chapter Ten

MY ADVENTURE WITH GOD

I t was December 20, 1974, and I was awakened by God at three-thirty am. The Lord spoke these words unto me: "Pack up your family and go to Colorado. Be out of Virginia in twenty-four hours." By that time, our family included our two baby daughters, Wanda and Lorraine. I wanted to look up and ask if I could talk to someone else, but instead I woke my wife and informed her that we must leave our new home, with its new trees growing taller in the yard, and with grass so green and soft that if you walked on it, I would know your foot print. My wife looked at me and said to go to an all-night grocery store and get all the boxes I could. The neighbors and the community came over to help us pack our U-Haul truck. I can still remember the neighborhood children asking us over and over if they could go with us.

I called my mother and shared our mission and she said, "God will be with you." I called my mother-in-law and she said, "Negro, you are crazy!" I couldn't fault her reaction because it was natural, and it did seem crazy! I went to see my pastor, because my mother-in-law had called him, and his response to me was, "You should wait until you have everything in order and know someone in Colorado that can help you." As I sat there listening to him talk, the Lord said into my ears, "Don't listen to him. I fired him years ago." I contacted my spiritual mother, Martha Dennis, with whom I would go to spirit-filled Sunday night church services. She prayed for the journey.

41

We loaded up the truck and around midnight, our youth singing group and leaders followed us almost to Richmond Virginia. They hated to see us go and as the neighborhood cried tears, they assured us they would take care of our home until we got it sold.

It was five days before Christmas and here we are in a U-Haul truck with all we could fit into it, going across country to a state we had never been to nor did we know anyone there. As we drove down the highway, we had this immense feeling of being very free and happy to simply please the Lord.

The truck was a straight stick and Marie couldn't drive a straight stick, so I would get it in the right gear and she would slip under me and drive for a few hours. This trip from Virginia to Colorado was 1,800 miles one way, but we were happy as we traveled across country.

When we reached Kansas City, Missouri, we were thinking we were close to Aurora, Colorado. We didn't realize it was still an eight-hour drive from Kansas to Aurora, Colorado. We also didn't know that all of Colorado was experiencing a record blizzard snowstorm. It was really blinding and slow all the way down the highway. We were literally driving by faith.

When we were about three hours from Aurora, in my rear view mirror, I saw a car swerve off the road and go down an embankment. I pulled off the road as best I could, trying not to endanger my wife and baby daughters. I ran back and fell down the embankment. Once I was near the car, I pulled a dazed man out of his vehicle back up the snowy hill. We pulled and pushed him into our truck to get him warm. We drove him to the next exit and called for the police.

We looked at this as a test, like the Good Samaritan story in the Bible. The parable of the Good Samaritan is a parable told by Jesus in the Gospel of Luke chapter 10, where a man who was traveling was stripped of his clothing, beaten, and left half dead alongside the road. The first person to come upon him was a priest, and then a Levite comes by. Levites provided assistance to the priests in the worship in the Jewish temple. However, both the priest and the Levite avoided the man; they passed him by. Finally, a Samaritan happened upon the injured man. Even though Samaritans and Jews despised each other, the Samaritan helped the injured man. Jesus told this parable in response to the question from a lawyer who asked, "And who is my neighbor?" In response, Jesus told the parable, letting the listeners know the real neighbor figure in the parable was the man who showed mercy to the injured man—that was the Samaritan. Yes, as the man who we helped out of the snow-filled embankment said, we could have easily passed him by but because of the Lord's love in our hearts, we became the Good Samaritan in his life. To God be the glory!

We continued on our journey, after helping this stranger, and arrived in Aurora, Colorado around nine pm on December 23, 1974. It was two days before Christmas. I found a phone booth, looked through the phone directory, and found the name of a man that my brother-in-law told me was a believer when he was stationed in the Air Force in Colorado. Amazingly, he answered my call and I told him about our journey. I asked if he could tell us where there was some reasonable housing. He asked me to describe our location, then said hold on for a minute and put his wife on the phone. As she was talking to us for about thirty minutes, we looked up and this short, white man was standing outside the phone booth, asking if we wanted to come and spend the night at his home. At first, I said no, but he was persistent. So we followed him to his house and met his wife. After taking much-needed showers, we went to bed in their warm home.

In the morning, I went to the living room and found seven, white, Christian men sitting in a circle. I found out later that they were all very well off financially. I shared my testimony about our call to Colorado. They shared how they put their money together into the building of a Christian nursing home, Sable Care Center. They had also been fasting and praying for God to send a chaplain for the nursing home. They shared that as they fasted and prayed, simply asking God to send the man they needed, they never thought about the color of the man nor where the man would come from. To God be the glory! I was the man they had been fasting and praying for. I became the chaplain at Sable Care and preached on Sundays. We were on our adventure with God!

Marie and I found an apartment and I started searching for a permanent job. I went to New York Life Insurance Company and became their Number #1 salesman in just sixty days. You remember I had honed my salesman skills as a teen in Hampton, Virginia.

Things were going well!!! We were settling into our new life in Colorado with an apartment and new job. Life was going well. It was almost like the time when we had gotten our new home in Hampton, Virginia. I had graduated from Norfolk State University, had a good job in the Newport News Shipyard, and things were going well. So, here we were in the same scenario in Colorado.

Then one day, the top man at our New York Life Insurance office, Mr. Redman, called me into his office. He said, "John, have a seat." I sat down, not knowing what this man was going to say. He leaned forward and then leaned back in his chair. He said, "John, I am a Christian and the Lord woke me up last night and told me that I have to share this with you. I have to tell you this." He got up from behind his desk and came and stood before me, and looked me straight in my eyes to say, "John, the Lord told me to tell you that you are supposed to be selling **ASSURANCE, not INSURANCE.**" My response to his statement: I immediately quit my job at New York Life Mutual Insurance and asked God what He wanted me to do beside preach on Sundays at the Sable Care Nursing Home.

Some of the wealthy men that we met since we arriving in Colorado were: Jim McKinney, who was a realtor; Ed McKenna, who was also a realtor; Dale Morris, owner of a coffee company; Adolph Coors, son of the Coors brewery founder; Arch Decker, who was a lawyer and realtor; Gilman Hill, who owned oil and gas leases and was also an inventor and geologist, along with his wife Vonnie Hill, were used by the Lord to bless us. They started taking me around and introducing me to preachers in the area.

I soon was invited to meet some of the local black pastors of Denver. I met Acen Phillips, A.L. Bowman, Barcus Adams, Harrell Alexander, and Wendell T. Liggins, as well as others. I shared my testimony with them and they were also moved about my adventure with God. One of the black pastors I met, Willard Johnson, asked me to go with him to a white Bible college, the Conservative Baptist Theological Seminary, known today as Denver Seminary. Willard shared how he remembered when he couldn't get into the seminary because he was black.

We set up an appointment to meet with the seminary president, Dr. Vernon Grounds. After hearing my testimony, he said he would love to have an African-American with my background to attend his school. He wanted a black brother that would bring more black students to the school and get more African American pastors to attend.

They took me into the school, with no money to enroll with and no Bible college degree. Dr. Vernon Grounds said he knew God would give me finances, since I had faith to come from so far. He told me I would learn quickly once I entered into the classes. I had to think hard about going to a predominant white seminary because my pastor, A.L. Bowman, and some other black pastors didn't want me to go there, but I was game. Pastor Barcus Adams convinced me to go with him to the Veterans of Administration office and they were so impressed with my life story that the intake agent asked if I had any injuries while in the military, since I had used my GI Bill to get my bachelor's degree in business administration from Norfolk State. I shared about my cut tendinitis and he put in the paperwork, requesting retroactive disability money. I was granted the disability money, which allowed me to not only get a nice monthly check, but I could buy the books I needed from the school bookstore for my classes. The intake agent told me later that after I left his office, he also invited Christ into his life.

I was sitting in this school with people from all types of denominations. They were teaching about a man named Martin Luther, which I thought they were talking about Dr. Martin Luther King Jr. Some of the students and staff were on the subject of Calvinism and Armenians' positions. They even talked about the swoon theory of whether Jesus was dead or asleep in the grave. I told them that I could never have these discussions in my neighborhood. They went on to discuss about their different positions on the return of Christ: was it pre-trib, mid-trib, or post-trib? I thought I would share my position on the return of Christ. I told them I was pan-trib. They asked me what that was, so I told them I was pan-trib because it would all pan out in the end. That is why we should not sit around arguing, but instead go out sharing the gospel. Of course, I was the thorn in their side because I wasn't believing all their foolishness. They even said that miracles, healing, and tongues were no more, but I told them that the Holy Ghost was still alive and well and still working through those methods. They tried for three years to change my thinking, but I remained with the mind of Christ!

I just kept studying about the Man in the red letters of my Bible. God can teach the pure in heart better than the pure in head. He is the one who saved me in Panama. It was the Man in the red letters who spared my life when I left the Black Panther Party in Panama. It was the Man in the red letters who kept me alive in Vietnam and brought me back home alive to my family. It was the Man in the red letters who woke me up and told me to be out of my hometown in twenty-four hours and to travel 1,800 miles across the country to a place unknown to me, my wife, and baby daughters. I knew that miracles were real and it didn't matter if these people had as many degrees as a thermometer; no one could convince me otherwise about the God I served.

I remember some white students in seminary said they wanted to come into urban ministry and be used of God. They were raising money to come and set up their own denominational churches. I told them that they should just go and join a black church, and let love get them in position to make a difference. How are you going to win people unless you join them? That's how I got to know the history of most of the sixty different denominations. I enrolled into a white school and I really got an understanding of how we took a simple gospel and made it complicated. Jesus came down from heaven to mingled among us, give His life as a ransom for our sin and challenged us to take the gospel message throughout the world.

I was doing chaplaincy work at the Denver jail during the week and traveling monthly to minister at the Canon City Prison, which was 113 miles away with the great evangelist Mae Buchannan. She was a mentor and one of the most excellent and anointed women I have ever heard preach and live what she was preaching. On one occasion, I was asked to travel to Canon City with Adolph Coors and other men to help Adolph meet the man, Joseph Corbett Jr., who robbed and killed his father as he was going for his morning walk. Since I was a known and respected chaplain in the Denver jails, they wanted me to talk Corbett into meeting with them. Adolph wanted to let Corbett know that he was concerned about his soul. Corbett wouldn't meet with him, so Adolph Coors left some material for him to read concerning the Word of God.

My wife and I were offered a job to be the night managers of an apartment building for single parents. It took up one block, had six floors, and was on Gilpin Street in Denver, Colorado. We took it on and there were 92 single parents with 130 children. It was more of a ministry than a job. We held Bible studies and kept things in order. The mothers were very upset that the fathers of the children could pick them up for the weekend to stay with their girlfriends, who made the children feel special. This brought anger out of the mothers during the week, when their children bragged about these women and all they did for them. We had to be on guard at all times to make sure the mothers weren't abusive. I believe that the fathers should have the child during the summer, to see that there is more to it than just picking up the child on Friday and not seeing all the work that has to happen during the week.

I remember one night, the father of one child came into the secured building to fight one of the mothers. I received a call in my apartment that the women on the fifth floor had trapped a man and were beating him badly with pans. I walked up the steps slowly, without using the elevators, and saw the women had taken out their anger and frustration on him. He had bumps all over his head before being arrested. I even got an old car, pulled it around the back of our building, and let the mothers come out and beat on the car to release their frustrations. That vehicle went from an old used car to just junk in a short time.

Denver Seminary Graduation & Horseback Riding in Colorado

Chapter Eleven

THE CALL TO FULL-TIME PRISON MINISTRY

I finished Conservative Baptist Theological Seminary in 1974. My new friends, who were like family, made airline reservations and flew my father, mother, and godmother, Lottie Bryant, to my graduation. They had never flown and were excited to meet all the new brothers and sisters in Christ I had.

They had a cookout for my family. I had told my dad to wear relaxing clothes and not try to impress them because they were humbled believers in Christ.

My father came outside dressed for church and was telling them how he was big landowner. I pulled my father aside and told him that it wasn't necessary to try to impress them because they were believers in Christ. He also knew that he owned just three, small lots!

We had a marvelous week together and were all so glad I followed the voice of God and drove those 1,800 miles across the country to Colorado. If I had stayed in Virginia, working in the Newport News Shipyard, I would have been one of those many men I worked beside who died from the asbestos and other chemicals that were discovered in the shipyard. There were many lawsuits and the asbestos had been in the departments for years.

49

After graduating from seminary, I learned there were no black churches hiring a young, black man with a wife and two children. There were inquiries from other Christian organizations: some of them included Young Life, Campus Crusade, Youth with a Mission (YWAM), and Prison Fellowship. My heart didn't want to leave my Black community, but pour back into people, especially the African-American community, all that I learned in school.

Three times I was asked by Chuck Colson, President of Prison Fellowship to be his North East director. Charles Wendell Colson, who was referred to as Chuck Colson, is best remembered for his role in the Watergate scandal. He served as special counsel to President Richard Nixon from 1969 to 1970 and was once known as President Nixon's "hatchet man." He was named as one of the Watergate Seven and pleaded guilty to obstruction of justice when attempting to defame Pentagon Papers defendant Daniel Ellsberg. He served seven months in the federal Maxwell Prison in Alabama. He was the first members of Nixon's administration to be incarcerated for Watergate-related charges. In 1973, he accepted Christ in his life and then dedicated his life to ministering to prisoners. Chuck approached me for the position with Prison Fellowship because he wanted a black man who would be always real with him and who would help him to get into the prisons to reach minorities. He wanted to set up groups all over America to support prisoners upon their release from prison. Helping them get housing, jobs, and church families.

Upon accepting the position in 1974, Chuck and I traveled together for about a year. We would go and study with great theologians, such as R.C. Sproul, and be a part of religious think tanks, etc. I still have memories of debating with Chuck; however, we never got to the point of disrespecting each other. God continued to give me favor in the prisons and communities, as I was setting up places for Chuck to speak. Staffers were added, and those at Prison Fellowship were taking the country by storm. Different races were coming together in this ministry to prisoners.

I remember one day, while I was setting up a seminar in Lorton Prison, just on the outskirts of Washington, DC, when some well-known African-American spiritual leaders approached and questioned me about going around the country with a white man.

I told them I hadn't noticed Colston color because **"It's not about skin, but sin."** "Brothers," I said to them, "if we are supposed to be about getting this gospel out into the world, what difference does it make who we get it done with?" I told them they needed to just figure out why Sunday morning in America is the most segregated day of the week. Some followers of Jesus Christ think the way of changing people's hearts is to work for a political party; however, only a relationship with Jesus Christ can change a person's heart. Behind the walls of our prisons, one will find the real church of Christ.

I was asked to go to Pennsylvania to set up a week of discipleship training at a local jail. During the week of training the inmates in disciples, the warden gave his life to Christ. I got a call from the commissioner of the prisons, and he wanted me to come to Harrisburg, Pennsylvania to explain what happened to his golfing partner (the warden). After arriving to see him, one hour later, the commissioner gave his life to Christ. That opened up opportunities in all the state prisons in Pennsylvania, and that's how God blessed us to go forth. I was also invited to come and address their annual wardens and chaplain meeting.

There was one occasion when I had scheduled Chuck Colson to come and speak in Covington, Virginia. The meeting place was packed with news agencies, reporters, and cameras from as far as Richmond, Virginia. I went to the small airport in Covington, along with a well-known citizen of the town, Shirley Bruffey, who had been ministering in the Alderson West Virginia Federal Prison for years. She was excited that Chuck was coming to validate what she and other volunteers were doing in the women's prison.

We were sitting at the airport, waiting for Chuck to arrive, and found out the flight was late. I called the headquarters of Prison Fellowship to inquire about where Chuck was and discovered there had been a mistake about the date of his coming.

They had scheduled for him to come the next day, same time. When I told what they said happened back at headquarters, I could see Shirley Bruffey's look of shock and disbelief. With tears in her eyes, skin changing to different colors, she said, "John, how do we go and tell the hundreds of people and the news' stations that Chuck is not coming until tomorrow at noon?" I told her, "Shirley, we will just go into the meeting hall and explain the mix-up." She shook her head in disbelief. I could feel her concern and dejection. When we entered the building, I went first to the room where the press was set up to explain the mix-up. They looked at me and said they were going to follow me into the main hall and watch me try to explain this to all these people. Challenge on!

I walked into the room, filled with hundreds of people waiting to hear Chuck. I went to the microphone and asked for their attention. Picture the scene in your mind. I was the only black person in the room, and it was my task to tell them that the man of the hour, Chuck Colson, was not going to be there.

"Ladies and gentlemen," I began. "There has been a mix-up in the schedule and flight arrangements and Chuck Colson will be here tomorrow at the same time." There was chatter around the room and then someone in the audience shouted, "Tell us your testimony!" So, I did just that and surely the Lord was with me. Everyone in the room, with tears in their eyes, stood up and gave me a standing ovation. Someone shouted, "If Chuck can top this, we will all be back tomorrow."

To God be the glory, because everyone including the press came back the next day at noon. Chuck's message was well received, and I am still popular in Covington, Virginia. Glory to God! Challenge won!

As God was moving in a mighty way through the prison ministry, unfortunately a prideful, power-hungry, controlling man joined our staff and told us that the staff was praying too long. I guess we didn't organize and put time on the prayers like some people do. I didn't see anyone looking at his/her watch when I was asked to pray for them as the chaplain in Urgent Care. This man was a heathen saint who didn't realize that one must have the spirit of God in one's life to be effective in ministry, both in the prison and in the community.

People like him think it's about the "pure in head" but really, it's about the pure in heart. Men and women behind the prison walls can spot foolishness and insincere hearts a mile off. Prison doors were opening everywhere, and miracles were happening during our weeklong seminars in the prisons. The prison chaplains, wardens, and community loved what we were about and let us in.

We were even allowed to hand-select men and women from the federal prisons and bring them to our Washington, DC headquarters to train them how to go back and make disciples for Christ in the prisons where they were incarcerated. It was very successful and legislators on the Hill in DC got to meet and greet them, with many walking away with their hearts touched. We were really moving forward fast.

But here came the money-hungry "man" again with his hands in his pockets moving around his change. This was the mentality I remember seeing when I was young and what helped drive me to black militancy. Sometimes the man in charge would come with manipulative schemes, usually moving coins around in their pockets with their hands. When we were fasting and praying for donations, we had to send extra cars to get the mail. We needed not to be dishonest.

The next thing this individual wanted to do was to separate the large donors from the small donors and to bring the large donors onto the board of directors of the ministry. Over the years, I have been on many boards and, believe me, I've seen cheater on the golf course and in the board meeting rooms. I would rather be in the prison with the residents than with religious con artists. They are experts at quenching the Holy Spirit and visions from God.

There was a wealthy man who owned a chain of hotels, and he wanted to give a large amount of money to Prison Fellowship to get the gospel into the New England prisons. As I listened to this compassionate man, I spoke up and told him how I had been working in the

New England area and there were Christian ministries already in prisons. I told him about Chaplain Don Moeberger and how he and his wife had been doing a great work there for years. I suggested to the man that he should give at least half of the $100,000.00 to Don Moeberger's ministry, because he and his family had ex-inmates living in their home. The man thanked me for being honest and did just that. I really believe in heaven they were rejoicing over our integrity, but the rejoicing did not come down from the vice president of operations.

I got called into the vice president's office and was told that I should never have told the rich man about the other prison ministry. I am not going to say I couldn't believe what I was hearing because the statement fit the vice president's pattern. I stared him down with the old Black Panther look, and he immediately backed away from me.

He went to Chuck and told him that he couldn't control me, to which Chuck informed him, that's the reason he hired me. You see, the vice president didn't realize, I didn't get saved to have a religious crook with bible degrees make me dishonest. Sadly, I witnessed thirty-three good, godly people leave that prison ministry in tears; some were called by God to leave, while others just left because they were negatively treated. They call themselves the bruised reeds.

It wasn't until years later that this one man was found out and released. Unfortunately, the ministry lost some good workers for Christ because of how they were treated by this man. I learned that one can destroy a ministry by putting a power-hungry, devious person in power. Sometimes leaders cannot see the snakes among them until it's too late.

Chapter Twelve

JERUSALEM: THE CALL TO ISRAEL

T he telephone rang and it was my spiritual brother, Gilman Hill, who was one of the seven men sitting in the living room that day my wife and I arrived in Denver. I could hear the excitement in his voice, as he said, "Johnny, I am drilling an oil well on Mount Carmel in Israel!!!" He had submitted the necessary paperwork to drill and, after putting the Word of God in all the documents that needed approval, he requested me to come and pray over the oil well before they started drilling. I had been working so hard with Prison Fellowship and had been promoted to the National Director to motivate and get many volunteers across the nation. Things were going well, but I requested from Chuck to be off for three weeks to go and be with Gilman and his wife Vonnie in Israel.

We prayed over the oil well; all the while, the Arab and Jewish people observed the loving relationship between Gilman and me. We were asked to share our faith and go to different cities to share our testimonies. This was the beginning of a work of reconciliation and where our ministry of reconciliation began.

They loved and requested us to come to a Baptist school in Nazareth to speak to the whole school. As Gil and I walked onto the school grounds, there were a number of youths out in the yard. It was a beautiful, sunny day. When we walked across the basketball court, someone threw a basketball. I caught the basketball and from half-court, I casually threw the ball over my back without looking and swish...all net . . . it went in the basketball hoop! The youth on the playground went up in a roar. I was an immediate hit, and all the Arab and Jewish families wanted me to come and eat in their community. Gilman and I laughed for an hour when we got back to the hotel, because it was the greatest luck shot I have ever made with a basketball in my life. The Lord was with us.

It was in 1983 and while in Israel, God clearly spoke to me to come back to America and resign my position with Prison Fellowship. I had been scheduled for speaking engagements for the next three years, but I needed to be obedient to the voice of God. So, I came back, resigned, and gave up my corner office. I went back to Israel and helped to start Israel's first prison ministry for Arabs. I studied at the Holy Land Institute, now called the University of the Holy Land, in the city of Jerusalem. It was a blessing to walk the land where Jesus walked, and to study and experience the Middle East with its various cultures. The biblical text came alive!

I was welcomed all over Israel. In the Palestinian city of Ramallah, I spent time at an orphanage, bringing a dialogue between Arabs and Jews. I enjoyed being at a village outside Nazareth with Pastor Suhail Ramadan, who was a Baptist pastor who helped start the prison ministry. I started setting up American tours for Pastor Suhail Ramadan and Dr. Labib Mikhail, a Coptic pastor from Egypt, to show what reconciliation looked like. Dr. Mikhail would engage in apologetic debates with Muslims leaders and wrote over seventy books, using Scriptures to prove the errors of the Koran and the truths of the Word of God. Pastor Ramadan and Dr. Mikhail have transitioned to heaven since then. Dr. Labib, in his nation, would be equivalent to the respect Billy Graham had in America. He was once being investigated by his government and they had police to attend his teaching rallies. The men after listening to him several times went to their leader and said they couldn't follow around with him anymore because he was convincing them to become believers. Upon Dr. Mikhail's death, his family gave our church library all the books he had written and published. What an honor and treasure!

The time I spent in Israel changed my life. Marie also got the opportunity to travel to Israel and study at the Holy Land Institute with my administrative assistant, Diane Lee. My time of studying the life of the Man in the red letters and walking the soil changed my entire understanding of Christianity and what it means to be a disciple of Christ.

Along with our ministry to Arabs and Jews, we were led by God to begin a counseling ministry, Reconciliation Fellowship, located in Fairfax, Virginia. It was through this ministry that we witnessed many families reconciled through the Word of God. Our clients consisted of individuals, couples, and families. We ministered to many who were not Christians, but the biblical principles made sense to them as they applied these principles to their lives. Many of my clients were white, but the color of my skin did not matter. They saw a man being used by God to bring healing in their lives.

Another part of the Reconciliation Fellowship ministry was a Christian radio program, on a local station, WABS/WAVA, where I was heard every Monday through Friday morning at 7:45. I was on the radio for over twenty-eight years! These years on the radio gave me an audience in the greater Washington, DC area. An interesting thing also happened to me one day, while I was on my way to the radio station. Just before getting on the interstate, I stopped at my local bank. As I got to the drive-up window, the bank teller told me that the bank had just been robbed and they were waiting for the police. I was told I could come back later. So, I left for the radio station and as I got on the interstate, I saw a lot of patrol cars coming behind me with flashing lights. I pulled over. Guns were pointed at my head. They snatched me out and searched me. I was asked where I had just come from and I told them the bank. They informed me that the bank had just been robbed and I was a suspect.

I was made to stand on the highway while we waited for the bank clerk to come and identify me. I heard later that my daughter was on a bus trip with her school and they passed me on the interstate. She noticed my car and was upset to see me being held by the police. The bank clerk eventually arrived, and she told them, "That is not the robber; that is Reverend Peyton!" She told them that the robber was five foot six and light-skinned; as you know, I do not meet that description. I breathed a sigh of relief and went on my way to the radio station. When I came home that evening, my daughter shared that she saw was on a school bus and saw me surrounded by the police and it was devastating to her. I am just thankful that the guns in my face didn't go off, but I am use to being targeted because of the color of my skin.

On another similar occurrence, I can remember at about eight pm one evening, when I was in Denver, that I got a call from Gilman and Vonnie Hill inviting me to come to their house. They lived in a very nice neighborhood. If you recall, they were one of the wealthy families I first met when I arrived in Denver. The policeman pulled me over to the side of the road in their white rich suburban neighborhood and asked why I was in the neighborhood. I told him where I was going, so he called the Hills and they came to my rescue. They felt my embarrassment and pain, and they protested very strongly to the manner of my treatment because this never happened to their white guests. They demanded that the policeman be fired; we know it today as racial profiling. A black, upstanding man is a dangerous species in America. If not for the grace of God, I would have been killed in America by now. The Vietnam Cong showed better kindness to me in 1968, when I was there fighting as directed by this government.

Israel!!!

Our "son" George Drayton who I met in
the orphanage in Ramla, Israel.

Chapter Thirteen

VOTED THE MOST LIKELY NOT TO SUCCEED IN HIGH SCHOOL TO PRESIDENT OF A BIBLE COLLEGE

I n 1994, I felt the call from God to continue my education in the pursuit of a doctorate degree in Christian counseling. After extensive searching and prayer, the Lord directed me to Carolina University of Theology, which was located in Belmont, North Carolina at that time. I enrolled into a dual program of the master's and doctorate of Christian Counseling Psychology program at Carolina University of Theology.

Carolina University of Theology was birthed in 1990, under the guidance of the Holy Spirit, to Dr. Gene Thompson and Dr. Joel Colette, Sr. These two men of God saw the need for quality Christian education for the busy pastor, evangelist, minister, or church worker who could not afford to pack up their family and travel to a Bible college or seminary. Their heart went out to the pastor who had been called to the small country church, and who knew he or she had the call, but had not been afforded the opportunity to continue their Christian education.

So, with a vision from God and a trust in His leading, Carolina University of Theology was born. The primary function of the university was to provide quality distance learning on a Bible college level.

Unlike the practices of most other countries, in the US, accreditation of institutions of higher education is not conducted by the government. The US government does not approve or accredit higher education programs and schools. Instead, it is a voluntary process that is implemented by private, nongovernmental accrediting agencies. At present, there are both regional as well as national agencies involved in the accreditation process. Even though accreditation is a voluntary act on the part of a university, Carolina University of Theology, in keeping with our desire to promote academic excellence, has had its accreditation with the Accrediting Commission International of Beebe, Arkansas since 1991. Accrediting Commission International is an international accrediting commission that holds at its primary objective the encouragement and maintenance of sound scholarship and the highest academic achievement in the areas of private education. ACI's purpose is the preparation of quality education in private schools, colleges, and theological seminaries. It is a non-governmental body and makes no claims to be connected with the government. We are presently seeking another accreditation.

I approached the university's president, Dr. Thompson, about the possibility of Reconciliation Community Church becoming a satellite/extension campus for the University in the Northern Virginia area. I traveled to North Carolina to meet with Dr. Thompson and the staff of CUT, and from that meeting, the partnership with the university was born.

In 1995, when our church, Reconciliation Community Church, was still located at 1305 Jeff Davis Highway in Woodbridge, Virginia, the first classes of the northern Virginia campus of Carolina University of Theology were held. Soon after that, I was asked to be the keynote speaker at the graduation banquet of the University in Charlotte, North Carolina. For several years after, I was asked to be the speaker for the banquet.

In 1996, I completed the dual program and earned my master's and doctorate degrees from the Christian Counseling Psychology program.

Graduating from Carolina University of Theology with my wife Marie by my side and one of my spiritual mothers, Mamie Williams.

In 2000, I was given an invitation to serve on the board of Carolina University of Theology, which I accepted. Reconciliation Community Church was a satellite campus for the university in Manassas, Virginia since 1995.

In 2002, the Lord saw fit to bring Dr. Gene Thompson into His presence. The family contacted and asked me to be a part of the home-going service, which had been a request of the late Dr. Thompson.

Dr. Phyllis Thompson, the wife of the late Dr. Gene Thompson, begin serving as the president of Carolina University of Theology, serving through 2004. In 2004, the university board then elected me as the new president. The university's administrative offices were still located in Iron Station, North Carolina, but in 2004, the university board voted to move the entire location to Manassas, Virginia. We continued to service satellite campuses in Detroit, New York, Georgia, Korea, North Carolina, London, and Radford, Virginia.

In 2008, the university board and administration moved all students enrolled in satellite campuses into the distance learning program.

Since my election as the university's president, along with the university board's decision to relocate the university's administrative headquarters from North Carolina to Manassas, Virginia, in keeping with our desire to promote academic excellence, we deemed it vital to gain additional accreditation through a regional and national accrediting agency.

I am proud to also say that Carolina University of Theology is also a member of the Virginia State Director with International Association of Christian Counseling Professionals. Carolina University of Theology is a religious institution exempt from state regulation and oversight in the Commonwealth of Virginia, and is authorized to confirm the following degrees: bachelor of biblical studies as well as masters and doctors in Christian education, Christian counseling, ministry, and theology.

The university's online presence is also in partnership with Sycamore campus to provide our students in one central online location for their college management/learning management system needs.

Chapter Fourteen

ANSWERING THE CALL TO BE AN UNDER-SHEPHERD TO THE SHEPHERD'S SHEEP: THE CALL TO PASTOR

After many years of having a successful counseling ministry, in 1984, I sought God's leading about pastoring a church and helping people to be true disciples for Christ. I walked and prayed every morning with three brothers in Christ: Larry Dennis, Allen Jones, and James Mason. I boarded a plane to Colorado and prayed in my spiritual quiet spot with a view of the magnificent mountains of Colorado. It was there that God told me to go back to Virginia and be an excellent pastor. I needed to be a straight stick in this crooked world. He made me realize that many are in the church loving the pastor more than the Master. Some pastors enjoy getting the glory that belongs to Christ. How will pastors explain to our Heavenly Father why they took the glory that belongs only to the Father, Son and Holy Ghost?

My family were faithful members of First Baptist Church of Merrifield in Merrifield, Virginia. After seeking God and informing the new pastor that God was leading me to start pastoring, Marie and our three daughters were given a great celebration dinner. I didn't want anyone from First Baptist of Merrifield to come with us to the new church we were forming, Reconciliation Community Church, because I wanted to leave honorably. We left with the church's blessing.

We started out with fifteen people at our home having a Bible study. We enjoyed growth and it wasn't long before we used the neighborhood club house and next had to rent an auditorium in Woodbridge High School for the study. We were under a time restraint, so there were many Sundays where we had to finish worshipping God in the parking lot. His presence was moving in a strong way, but we were obedient to the time given. We would pretend that the empty chairs in the auditorium were filled with future members, and we would turn and wave at the empty chairs and welcome the new people who would be filling up those seats.

The school's assigned maintenance man and wife were Christians – Favor! This elderly couple were so moved by the spirit in our services that they not only let us go over our time, but allowed us a place to store our equipment so we wouldn't have to take it with us after each Sunday service. Favor!

As we grew, it was time to move again. We left the high school and moved into an office complex on Jefferson Davis Highway, Route #1 in Woodbridge, Virginia. We were next door to an Allstate Insurance Company that was owned by two businesswomen who happened to be sisters. These two ladies admired us and the kindness we showed to them. They didn't see our color, but saw our character and trusted us enough to let us use their office space for some of our Sunday school classes. It became so tight in the main area where we held service that we would hit hands in the air when we praised God.

After knocking down walls in our office space to enlarge the room where we held our services, we settled down and enjoyed having a place to worship without time restraints. We were asked by the owner of a local car dealership, Woodbridge Jeep, if we wanted to use his dealership for service. Before we could say yes, the owner decided to buy a house, which he renovated and converted into a church for us to use. He told me to pay monthly what I wanted. He then laid out gravel for a parking lot so we could park without getting mud on our feet when it rained. He installed big lights outside the building, so we could have lights when we came to services at night. He gave us turkeys to give away for Thanksgiving and a large deep freezer filled with frozen meats and vegetables to give out to those in need in the community.

This white brother in Christ didn't see our color; he saw the work we were doing in the city, such as counseling, giving away free food and clothing, and ministering weekly to the men incarcerated at the Lorton Correctional Complex prison in Lorton, Virginia, operated by the District of Columbia. We went there for over twenty years. This man also witnessed how we offered free GED classes to those in the community. So, in seeing all of this, God used him to bless us! Favor!

We journeyed from this location, which we called, **"The Little House on the Prairie,"** to a shopping center that gave us 10,000 square feet. We were excited!!!! In the shopping center building, we had on one side an auto parts store owned and operated by a brother in Christ, and on the other side was a restaurant owned and operated by a Muslim. On Thursday nights, the restaurant was transform into a club. They had "Soul Night" with a live band and a DJ. The parking lot would be jammed, so we would go fishing — fishing for lost souls.

We would stand out in front of our church or walk the parking lot to share Christ and pray for those entering or leaving the nightclub until two am. Many of those that attended were young church members partying. The Lord added to the church, as God blessed us to lead many into a relationship with Jesus. Favor again!

One day, the Muslim manager approached me and told me that I shouldn't get comfortable, because he was going to expand his bar right into our side of the building where we had our services. I looked him directly in the eyes and smiled. Politely, I informed him that my God was greater than his god. Challenge on!

We continued to treat everyone in the shopping with kindness, including a group of young hippies that lived behind us in the woods, sleeping in tents. We would allow them to come into our building and use the restroom and freshen up. We just showed them the love of Christ, realizing that every need is not our call.

One day, as we were sitting on our side of the building we were renting, the doorbell rang and it was the Muslim manager of the restaurant bar next to us. He came to me with tears in his eyes and told me he had just received a phone call from his boss, who was out on a boat somewhere in Florida, and he was instructed to close down the restaurant immediately and to offer to us anything we wanted in the restaurant.

When my wife and I went into the restaurant, we saw the employees all around the bar, standing in shock from the news and weeping. We consoled them but did as we were told to do, and we took the couches and all the bar stools, asking them to kindly get up from the bar stools as we carried them out. Believe me when I tell you that we took everything, except the many roaches. When the lights were brightened, it showed how filthy things were. Favor!

We declared all the grounds in that shopping center for the Lord and the shopping center was listed as the "Shopping Center Of The Year," in Woodbridge, Virginia. Our church was really growing, and we were paying the least amount of rent with the largest amount of space, including now the space where the Muslim's restaurant was.

One day, we looked up and saw construction equipment removing a big restaurant that was in the parking lot directly in front of our church. It kept blocking our church from being seen and was totally demolished in one day. Favor! Although we were grateful for the favor given to us in the shopping center, we really wanted a place to call our own. We started praying and believing God for land and a building.

We knew it was time for us to leave the shopping center and, by faith, did so. I remember the day when we walked around the shopping center and asked the Lord to allow the anointing, which was upon those grounds, to follow us to our new location.

You see, we would pray and anoint the doors of each of those businesses while we were tenants. When we left, the anointing that was upon those businesses left with us; it literally became a ghost of a shopping center.

We were asked by the pastors of two churches in Woodbridge, Rector John Guernsey of All Saint Episcopal Church and Pastor Charlie Chilton of Grace Baptist Church, if we would use their building until we had our own. Our answer was yes! Favor! We enjoyed being with them and we had great times together, especially during New Year's Eve when our churches would bring food and eat together. After the midnight service, our white brothers and sisters loved what we brought (collard greens, cabbage, steak, yams, chitterlings, pound cake, lemon meringue, etc.) They would bypass what they brought and eat what we brought.

Pastor Charlie Chilton wanted us to come and use their building because they knew that the history of the Southern Baptist denomination supported slavery and racism, and they wanted make reconciliation. As pastors, we would have our services in different locations on the grounds and some Sundays, we would exchange pulpits. He would preach to Reconciliation members using their fellowship hall and I would preach in the sanctuary to Grace members. We had joint picnics together at the church and in the local parks. Favor! I remember us using a park for Veterans Day but it was predicted to rain all day long. We went to the park and prayed that not one drop of water would fall while we were have a great fellowship. It rained outside of the park and not one drop of water fell on us. We watched a rainbow come across us and we lifted up our hands and praise the Lord.

Grace Baptist Church (Woodbridge, Virginia) also hosted a Filipino church who used their building in the afternoon. Pastor Charlie and his wife, Grace, were missionaries in the Philippines for over twenty-five years and they spoke the language fluently. When we started building our own church, I asked Pastor Charlie if I could use his old beat-up pickup truck and I would leave him with my car. He told me he couldn't be seen in my nice car because some of his members might get upset. We found out that they hadn't had a new vehicle for years and we were devastated. So, the Lord blessed our church to raise enough money and at Pastor Charlie's retirement celebration, our little congregation presented Pastor Charlie and his wife a brand-new Toyota truck, which he had always wanted. His wife, children, and grandchildren were over-joyed and drove around the parking lot after the retirement celebration.

When Pastor Charlie was dying of cancer, I called and asked if he wanted to preach at RCC, since he was retired. At first, he felt he couldn't muster up the energy, so I told Pastor Charlie that he *"should not die until he was dead."* Surely enough, on a Saturday night, he called and asked if he could preach one more time. Of course, I said, "yes." Pastor Charlie Chilton's members said that for over twenty-five years, someone gave his/her life to Christ almost every Sunday. His church would let him preach for about thirty minutes and we let him preach until he was preached out. We were shouting as he delivered the Word of God with Excellency! Favor!

I enjoyed pastoring; however, it hurt when people just came to get what they wanted to make their lives pleasant, and then they would find an excuse to leave, knowing there is no perfect church. It hurt at first, as we had people living in our home for seven years and some were not kind nor grateful, but we just kept helping. We moved over two hundred families into new homes and apartments, and just gave whatever we had in order to give people an opportunity to see the love of Jesus in action. We were doing all of this, while some were plotting on how to prove they could do ministry better than me. This was hurtful because some were preachers I trained.

Yes, it was painful and often heartbreaking, but we have stayed at Reconciliation Community Church because it is where the Lord has called us.

Pastor Peyton And Minister Marie Banner

Chapter Fifteen

ENLARGING OUR TERRITORY …
GETTING THE RIGHT LAND AND
BUILDING TO USE AS A TOOL FOR
KINGDOM WORK

W
e found ourselves like the children of Israel, looking for that land of promise to build what I have always called a tool for kingdom work. We kept looking and believing that different parcels of land were ours. We walked them, prayed over them, and asked God if this was the land of promise. Then we saw ten acres of land in Manassas, Virginia. I can remember when we drove out to the property how we literally thought we were going to a foreign land, because the land had not been developed. The route to the land was a two-lane road and at night, it was nothing but darkness. We set up a time to meet and talk to the owner of the property. Her property consisted of a rambler-style home, a horse farm, and a large barn that she had named, "Almost Heaven." Yes, that was the real name! There was a signpost with those words written on it near the barn and she wanted $500,000 for her land.

One Sunday after our morning service, our leaders were walking the land and the Holy Spirit said it was our land of promise. We started dancing and shouting unto the Lord, with hands lifted up and believing what the Lord was showing us.

Looking back now, it seemed like things started moving quickly after that. A white brother, believer and president of a bank, Dave Holden, had a model made of a church he thought we could afford. I rejected it because it was not what God told me to build. We were to build a multi-purpose building that would be a tool to be used for different functions. Dave came to a morning service and told the congregation we could, in no way, build what I was proposing and he would eat a cooked crow if it could be accomplished. We got the necessary papers from a local bank to complete in order to purchase the land. After we completed the paperwork, which included showing five years of our financial records, we presented the papers and the loan was approved. We had never met face to face with the bank personnel, so when I went to sign the final papers, the bank managers pulled me in a room and told me that I really tricked them because they didn't know we were a pre-dominantly black congregation. We had a laugh and became proud owners of ten acres of land, which ended up costing us only $100,000. Favor!

We had the land of promise, but we didn't stop there. I was sitting in a restaurant with my Italian Christian brother Ron Talerico, and we drew on a napkin what God had been showing me to build. The Lord showed me a 53,000 square foot, multi-purpose building with Jerusalem blocks (white brick) outside and a blue roof with a big cross on top.

I can remember how one night at our intercessory prayer time, when we were in the shopping center location, praying out to the Lord, how one of the intercessors that night started writing down what the Lord was showing me of how the building would look like on the inside and what rooms would be included.

It sounded easy when laying out the plan with Ron on a napkin, but after meeting with the architect, different contractors, and construction companies, we learned the building was going to cost $5.6 million and we had only $30,000 in the bank. Because I had taken that adventurous journey to Colorado, I knew the power of believing God and seeing the reality of living by faith. Even as a child, when my mother would sit us at the table in the kitchen with no food in the house, she would pray and there would always be a knock at the back door with a neighbor standing there with food. This had happened quite a few times, so as a result, I had come to know this God of my mother. I feared nothing once God spoke. Favor!

We were rejoicing unto the Lord for making a way for us to get ten acres of land to start building our tool for His `a8yt disciples to meet. I was told that there was a petition being circulated to keep us from building on the land. The community was being told that if we, as black people, came into the neighborhood, there was going to be robberies and rapes. A multitude of horrible things were said about us. There were white neighbors who said things like, "Over my dead body you won't build." Even our few white members were taken back by the comments. One of our black members was from Louisiana and he looked white. He would go and sit around the negative whites and report what they were saying. Even some of the young people in the neighborhood would tell us of their plans.

Marie and I sought the wisdom of God and decided to sell our six-teen-room home in Lakeridge, Virginia, and move our family into the small three-bedroom, rambler, ranch-style house on the grounds where we were going to build the church. Since we knew we were in God's will, we slept peacefully, all the while knowing that someone could shoot through our back room window. Racism hurts when being victimized. I remember when walking my daughters to school, the newspapers reporter recorded only the white men holding their children's hands, but never turn the camera to see black men walking their children. It took two years before the neighbors realized that we were godly people. As a matter of fact, the newspaper came and wrote an article about my life. It was then that the neighbors realized how I came to know Christ, and that I was a Vietnam Veteran and had been blessed by the Lord to be in what they considered high places in ministry across the country. We even had Adolph Coors IV to come and speak at a fund-raising dinner on our behalf.

In any promise that the Lord gives, there will always be opposition, just like the children of Israel when they went to spy out the land the Lord had promised them. Some saw giants, while two saw an opportunity for God to give victory. So, it was with us!

The neighborhood where our land was had no public sewage and many of the neighbors had the sewage running in the ditches, right in front of their homes. The county told us that a large portion of our property had to be designated for parking vehicles, and a portion had to be for our sewage drainage field. Many saw this as giants, but we said not so!

We believed that God was going to bring public sewage pipes to our land, but just not to our land but to the entire neighborhood. We contacted the local newspaper and was given an opportunity to share our story. An article was written in which we shared that it was a shame that the local animal shelter, less than one minute away, had public sewage but the human beings didn't. Then neighbor Mrs. Barbara Samsky, our church administrative assistant Dr. Carol Powell, and I went to Richmond, Virginia, and made some loving noise concerning the situation in the community. We were heard and we were rewarded! The decision was made to bring public sewage lines to our church and to any neighbor who wanted to attach on. The road was widened, and the sewage lines and pipes were put in. We became the neighborhood hero. Challenge won!!

Some neighbors even came and apologized to us. Even our next door neighbor, who had stood at the gate that separated our property when we moved into the house, told me that he didn't want us to live next door to him. After we were there three months, his wife asked if my wife would babysit his child until they could get a new sitter. He had my family over to his house and cooked a good piece of steak, put his arms around me, and told me we were the best neighbors he ever had. Favor!

Chapter Sixteen

BUILDING TIME – EXCEPT
THE LORD BUILDS THE HOUSE

W e called a meeting to bring together all the different people that would be needed to start building our 53,000-square foot, steel-frame building and none of them, including the project manager, asked about the funding source for our construction or about our construction loan. Each company or trade, as they call themselves in the construction field, started to bring their equipment onto our land, believing that we would be paying them after the work was completed. None of the builders asked for upfront money, with the exception of one who happened to be a minister of the gospel. He asked for $60,000 up front to do the excavation. After he was given the requested amount, a phone call came in from the pipe company that he had supposedly ordered the water drainage and sewage pipes from. They delivered them to our site, but they never paid for the pipes and the company was going to put a lien on our property. I was in utter shock and embarrassment, and immediately went to him.

When I talked with the preacher, he informed me that he put our money on another job site he was working at. We responded by paying again for the pipes, but directly to the pipe company and we asked for more professionalism from this brother in Christ. The potential violations while doing his job and consistent tardiness was slowing the project and could bring heavy fines from OSHA, the agency that could shut down the job. Knowing that these violations could cause death or serious injuries, along with the other contractors, we all sat down with him and shared our concerns. In anger, he came at night and removed all his construction equipment from our job site and just walked away.

We were in shock and could not believe this was happening right in the middle of our construction project, but God blessed us to get a better company the next day. It ended up costing us $150,000.00 to fix the mistakes he had left us with, but this wasn't the end of the story. We ended up getting a subpoena, because the preacher claimed we put him off the job. He failed to remember that we had documented his tardiness, unsafe practices, and what his delays were costing us.

To counter his false claim, five professionals in his field signed depositions that he had done the job wrong and when we were scheduled to go the court for his subpoena, all the evidence was in our favor and I knew we were going to win. However, the Lord spoke to me and said, "John, forgive him. Don't make him pay the $150,000.00 owed." No, I didn't look up to heaven and asked if there was anybody else up there I could talk to. I obeyed God and learned a very expensive lesson. I learned that there are "saints" and "ain'ts." Just because they have a fish on their cards doesn't make them true Disciples of Christ.

The unbelievers doing the construction work had great integrity and we had no more disputes with any of them. Many of the workers came to us daily asking for prayer for themselves and their families. Everything was going fast, and the trucks came rolling in to dig out the foundation of the basement area of our building, and then a knock came on our door at the house.

A white mother gave us $20,000. She shared that she was giving us this $20,000 because we led her drug-using daughter to Christ in the local jail where we had been ministering every week for over twenty-eight years. Favor! A week later came a black man with a certified check for $52,000 to give us because he heard we were building, and he was touched that I had driven long distance to his mother's funeral. Favor!

One morning, we were needing $71,000 toward the purchase of the steel. We had to have the money in the bank by 11:00 the next morning. I sat up all night on a tractor praying. Would you believe my Daddy delivered the money on time? We were paying as we watched the building going up.

The construction workers, the architect, the steel engineer, and the civil engineer loved our attitudes, and many still keep in touch with us today. Some have asked us to do the home-going services for their loved ones, while some still send every year a few thousand dollars to our ministry. It has been over twenty years!

Except the Lord builds the house became a reality to us. Psalm 127:1-3 says, "Unless the Lord builds house, the work of the builders is wasted. Unless the Lord protects the city, guarding it with sentries will do no good." We knew it had to be the Lord's doing because on paper it looked impossible, but we serve a God who can do anything but fail. I was led of God to ask those called by Him to be members of Reconciliation Community Church, to enter into a time of fasting and praying for forty days. I thought surely they would kill me, but they all agreed. We fasted from all meats and could only have liquid substance and daily prayed together. After twenty-days of fasting, there was no food left in our bodies. Our bodies felt great and our senses were increased. Our prayer life became more powerful.

As we were fasting and praying, I got a call from a man who owned Kings Pharmaceutical, who was on the board of a prison ministry with me. He asked what I was up to, because he admired how I carried myself at the board meetings and he could see Christ in my life. I told him I was believing God to help us build our building debt-free. I explained to him that a banker met with our congregation on a Sunday morning and told us that we could not build what we had on our architectural drawing. He knew what was in our bank account, so it would be an unbelievable feat if we did build that building. However, if we did, he said he'd come and eat a cooked crow on a Sunday morning.

He told the congregation that I was crazy, but he was willing to help us if we built the little church he had designed. Well, everyone laughed, for you see we were fasting and praying for the miracle, which was a debt-free building that God had shown me. *Except the Lord Builds the House!!!*

John Gregory of Kings Pharmaceutical invited my wife and I to his office in Bristol, Virginia. In his board room, he said God had spoken to him to help us. We were given a check for $250,000 and 20,000 shares of their stock. My wife and I were praising God as we drove back to Manassas, Virginia. Favor! He also, at the same time, gave a prison ministry 20,000 shares. The stock was selling for $8.00 a share, and the stock could go up and down in price. The board of the prison ministry sold their stock for $8.00, but the Lord told me to wait for Him and to keep fasting and praying, which is just what we did.

About thirty days later, the stock went up to overnight to $46.00. My broker called and he was excited, trying to get me to hold out longer, but the Lord told me to sell and we did. Five days later, the stock went back down to $8.00. Favor! *Except the Lord Builds the House!!!*

I received a call from John asking what I had done with the stock he and his brother gave us. I told him how we were fasted and prayed and that God told me to wait. By waiting, we were able to receive $46.00 per share! He told me that he was sending 20,000 more of his stock, and for me to call and tell him how the Lord was directing us.

We rejoiced and laughed, as we were paying our bills on time. As soon as the inspectors approved something, we paid. The contractors were emotionally moved by the fact that we paid them without them having to secure a construction loan that possibly could take up to thirty days to get paid. They gave us 15-20 percent off on some of our bills.

I remember the county planning and zoning commission wanting to know why we were going to put a large, lit-up cross on the top of our building. They said most of the churches put up a simple steeple with a small cross on top. I explained that my leader, Jesus Christ, died on a cross, not a steeple. They liked the boldness I had for my Christian beliefs. *Except the Lord Builds the House!!!*

All was going so well, and then God called us to another time of fasting and praying. This time, He instructed us to enter into thirty days of fasting and prayer like before. In the middle of the fast, the stock went up from $8.00–$52.00 overnight. I called Brother John and he said thanks, so we cashed in and sure enough a week later, it fell back down to $8.00. John followed our example and made over 100 million dollars. *Except the Lord Builds the House!!!* I think they were questioned about having an insider, but little did they know that the insider was JESUS! Favor!

Our Episcopal and Grace Baptist friends came over and helped us paint the building. Another pastor, Rev. Enoch Butler, gave us his ceiling lights and a baptism pool. Love poured in from everywhere because it was **the Lord building His House**.

Our newly constructed building wasn't totally complete at the time of the dedication. We still had carpet that needed to be put down and lights to be installed in classrooms. People, from the rich to the poor, of all nationalities came locally and from across the nation to our dedication. We had a glorious time, as brothers and sisters celebrating what the Lord had done. That is why our church logo is a black hand and white hand joining together to make a cross.

Why don't more work together as the Body of Christ? **Ego – Edging God Out**.

Would you believe that a group of denominational people put out that we were selling drugs in order to get the money we needed to construct our church, just because we experienced a miracle from God? One of the pastors, before he died, called me and apologized. He said God told him how wrong he was to bother with a man who lives by faith, not a religion of faith. We had a joint reconciliation service and I, again, told how God did it. Favor!

Except the Lord builds the House!!! We have been in our debt-free building for over twenty years. Many have used our building for funerals, weddings, conferences, baptisms, and for overnight stays for youth coming to the Washington, DC area for youth conferences.

Do you remember that white congregational church in my home-town of Hampton, Virginia, that was twenty-eight steps from my home church, and how they wouldn't let us visit them because we were told blacks were not welcomed? Well, the youth from that church uses our building to stay in when they come to Washington DC for youth con-ferences. They have no clue what their parents did to black people in Hampton, Virginia. Things have really changed!

We once had ten to twelve full-time staff members at our church. We continue to look forward to our mission trips to Haiti, Ghana, Uganda, and Honduras. We have been blessed to lead study pilgrimages/tours to Israel. We continue to minister in nursing homes, county jails, feed the poor, and give away free clothes, etc.... At the writing of this book, I am again the co-chairman of the Prince William Ministerial Association. I am believing God to build a city on two thousand acres of land to house two hundred-and-fifty senior citizens, un-wed mothers, bat-tered spouses, and troubled teens. We plan to build for our Bible col-lege, its own free-standing facility, which will include dorms. We will also build a new worship sanctuary, a 200-room Empowerment campus for men and women released from jail, and an assisted living facility for the elderly. We will again be debt-free and will focus on ministering love, not making a profit off the suffering of others. I can honestly say that I love pastoring and even now, I have in our building, four gener-ations of our family, working and serving the Lord daily. I am a blessed man whose steps have been ordered by the Lord. "**The Lord directs the steps of the godly. He delights in every detail of their lives.**" (Ps. 37:23). **Favor!**

Rcc Church History

Rcc Construction

This is not the end of my story . . . for the best is still yet to come!!!!

Peyton Family

Four generations...

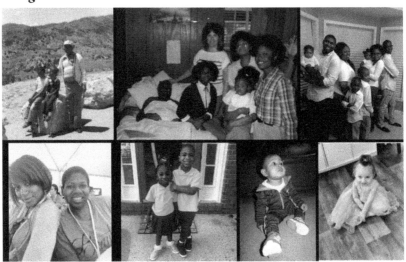

Four Generations

*The title of this book, **Have You Seen My Daddy?**, came about because, all of the adventures you have read about in my life never included my biological father. However, I have an "Abba," which, in the Greek New Testament, translates to "daddy." I have always sensed the presence of somebody directing my steps in life. When I came into the knowledge of the Trinity, I realized that my Heavenly Father/Daddy was with me and had a great destiny for me, and He would always be with me. My Daddy told me that not only would my family come into the knowledge of Him, but that I would leave a legacy and an inheritance for my family. He is the best Daddy you can have in life!*

In HIS Service,

X John R. Peyton
Servant of Jesus Christ

My family at Inner Harbor, Maryland 2018

85

CPSIA information can be obtained
at www.ICGtesting.com
Printed in the USA
LVHW072042290920
667401LV00014B/2503